IMAGES
of America

AROUND SISTERS

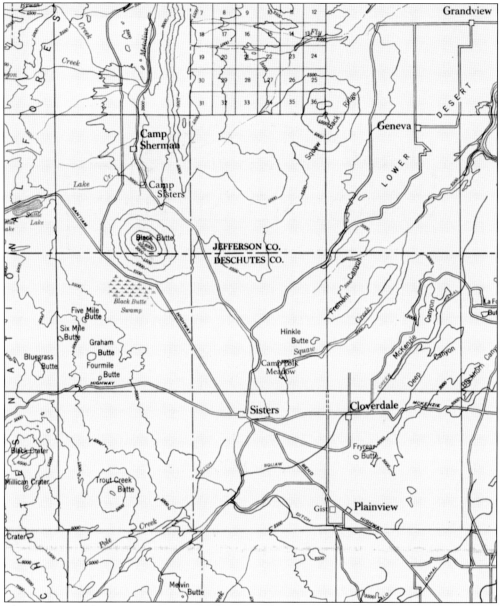

This is a map of the Sisters area in Central Oregon. (Courtesy of the Bureau of Reclamation, US Department of the Interior.)

ON THE COVER: In 1910, this photograph of the Smith family was taken in front of their general store and post office on Cascade Street. From left to right are Eliza Taylor Smith with daughter Mable, Robert holding baby daughter Bonnie, and Robert's brother Alex. Sitting in front are sons Harvey (left) and Hugh. The group of people down the street are citizens of Sisters. Robert and Alex Smith founded Sisters, Oregon, in 1901. (Courtesy of Oregon Historical Society.)

IMAGES
of America

AROUND SISTERS

Sharon E. Karr

ARCADIA
PUBLISHING

Published by Arcadia Publishing
Charleston, South Carolina

Printed in the United States of America

Library of Congress Control Number: 2024931287

For all general information, please contact Arcadia Publishing:
Telephone 843-853-2070
Fax 843-853-0044
E-mail sales@arcadiapublishing.com

Visit us on the Internet at www.arcadiapublishing.com

To my sister, Kathryn A. Karr,
who is always supportive, understanding, and eager to assist

CONTENTS

ACKNOWLEDGMENTS

I want to express my gratitude to the numerous individuals who have assisted by providing photographs and sharing information for this book, *Around Sisters*. I am incredibly grateful to the Crook County Historical Society and Bowman Museum historian Steve Lent for reviewing my book proposal and providing the initial images to begin this project. Rebekah Averette and Vanessa Ivey of the Deschutes County Historical Society were instrumental in advising me about researching the comprehensive photograph collection at the Des Chutes Historical Museum. The Three Sisters Historical Society and several others associated with the Sisters Museum encouraged and supported this project. Scott Daniels at the Oregon Historical Society Research Library was also incredibly helpful in finding all the folders and boxes I requested, offering additional research suggestions, and pursuing avenues I had yet to consider.

I also want to thank the descendants of local pioneer families and businesses, government agencies, and utility companies who willingly shared photographs and provided unique history about Sisters.

Selecting the most suitable photographs from the numerous ones available to showcase the story of Sisters accurately and engagingly was a challenge. It required defining what makes Sisters unique, from its early history to the growth of this small town with thousands upon thousands of tourists passing through each season.

Several people read the text and offered input that clarified the information, and I want to thank them: Kathryn Karr, Zeta Seiple, and Gary Kish. My editor at Arcadia Publishing, Caitrin Cunningham, answered my questions and provided recommendations, guiding this book to successful completion. Lastly, I am grateful to my family and friends, who patiently listened to my endless tales about Sisters while researching the material for this book.

Many other contributors are recognized in the individual photograph credit lines, including Deschutes County Historical Society (DCHS), Three Sisters Historical Society (TSHS), Deschutes National Forest–Sisters Ranger District (DNF-SRD), Crook County Historical Society (CCHS); Oregon Historical Society (OHS), and Camp Polk Pioneer Cemetery Preservation Committee (CPPCPC).

INTRODUCTION

Sisters began in a scenic, lush meadow a few miles northeast of the current town. Camp Polk Meadow is an area visited for thousands of years by native tribal groups from the Columbia River to the north and the Great Basin to the southeast. The Columbia River influence included the Wasco people, and from the Great Basin came the Northern Paiute people. Additionally, tribes from the west, along the Cascade foothills, may have used the meadow and Whychus Creek. The native people gathered, and families for generations revisited the same locations, which provided a rich resource for food and water. This acknowledgment of the area's early history around Sisters is done out of respect for the indigenous caretakers of these lands and waters who lived here before the first settlers arrived. There are no known photographs and only a few drawings of those early times, which are better represented in books that are not photograph-based, such as this book, *Around Sisters*.

In 1865, a contingent of Oregon soldiers crossed east over the Cascade Mountains from the Willamette Valley, set up headquarters in a meadow along Whychus Creek, and named it Camp Polk, after the location of Capt. Charles LaFollette's home in Polk County, Oregon. Captain LaFollette, the military leader who established this encampment with the volunteer infantry, was given instructions to subdue "Indians" who were harassing settlers. A parade ground was cleared, and log cabins were built for housing. The contingent departed in the spring of 1866 and returned west over the Cascade Mountains to the Willamette Valley, having had no encounters with Native Americans.

Before this, there was minimal exploration or settlement of the area around Sisters. The Lewis and Clark Expedition passed to the north along the Columbia River, as did the Oregon Trail migration of wagon trains starting in 1842. Fur trappers who worked their way into the mountains from the North Santiam passed through. Among this group was Joseph Gervais, who arrived in Oregon in 1812 to work for John Jacob Astor and later with Hudson's Bay Company. He established his farm on French Prairie, near today's Gervais, Oregon. Explorers were among the earliest people who traveled through the region, including John Fremont and Kit Carson in 1843.

The Cascade Mountains were challenging to cross, keeping the Willamette Valley settlers from coming east to this unknown part of Oregon. In 1845, scouting for a road over the Cascade Mountains began in earnest but was years from reality. When gold was discovered in Idaho in 1859, traveling west-to-east over the Cascades started in earnest. As roads were built from the Willamette Valley to Central Oregon, a toll road was established between Cascadia, Oregon, and Cache Creek, near Suttle Lake, west of Sisters. Settlers began to head east in earnest as the early wagon roads neared completion. Sheep and cattle passed through the beginnings of Sisters on their way west to summer pastures in the mountains and returned through Sisters to winter over on ranches to the east. Sisters supplied the stockmen and provided a stopping place to rest and replenish supplies.

In 1886, John J. Smith, from Linn County, Oregon, filed a homestead claim along the road from the Willamette Valley and east of the Cascade foothills where Sisters would begin. He opened a store, and the town officially started in 1888 when the post office relocated from the Hindmans' homestead at Camp Polk to Smith's store. The move necessitated a new name for the post office. The name "Sisters" was chosen because of the three imposing mountains seen in a panoramic view above the town, the Three Sisters.

John J. Smith sold out in 1898 to Alex Smith, no relation, from New Brunswick, Canada, who was a pioneer of Sherman County and engaged in raising sheep. Alex then sold half of his holdings to his brother Robert. On July 15, 1901, Alex and Robert Smith platted the original townsite. Sisters was described in *An Illustrated History of Central Oregon* as "a little town situated amid the most delightful pine forest to be found anywhere." By 1904, Sisters had two general stores, one hotel, a blacksmith shop, a saloon, a real estate office, a livery barn, a schoolhouse, and its first lumber mill. The first school was built in 1885, and a larger two-room school was built in 1890. By then, several small lumber mills were in operation around Sisters.

Moving forward 100 years to 2001, the Oregon State Legislature determined the name "squaw" was considered a disrespectful term for an Indian woman and needed to be removed from geographical features. In 2006, Squaw Creek, which passes through both Sisters and Camp Polk, was renamed Whychus Creek, a respected Native American name. *Around Sisters* uses Whychus for all historical references wherever possible.

This book offers a unique perspective on the history of Sisters, including its pioneers, loggers, educators, ranching families, and more who contributed to its growth. From its humble beginnings to its present-day status, Sisters has a rich story. Enjoy this journey through the perseverance and progress of pioneers to the enduring spirit of Sisters, Oregon.

One

CAMP POLK AND EARLY SETTLERS

With the discovery of gold in Eastern Oregon and Idaho, interest sparked among settlers in the Willamette Valley. As a result, the Native American trails were transformed into roads. One of these roads was the Santiam Wagon Road, which passed through Camp Polk and went east to Prineville, the largest town in Central Oregon at the time. During the Civil War, soldiers from Polk County assisted in building the final six miles of the road and were sent east to protect settlers from Chief Paulina. Although no incidents occurred, the soldiers wintered over at the newly named Camp Polk, north of the future town of Sisters, from September 1865 to May 1866 before being ordered back to the Willamette Valley.

By 1880, some families found the Willamette Valley too crowded, so they ventured east to the less populated Central Oregon. There were about six homesteads in the Sisters area at the time, with the Hindmans and Wilts residing at Camp Polk and brothers Marcus J. and John W. Wilt located southwest of Sisters; near Black Butte, the Grahams settled what would later known as Graham Corral; and south of town, Alfred Cobb established his ranch, later named the Lazy Z. The Carey Federal Irrigation Act in 1894 brought water to the area, attracting additional settlers. These pioneers traveled over the Santiam Wagon Road to Central Oregon in covered wagons.

Sisters became a popular stopping point for travelers of all types, including cattlemen, sheepherders, and fur trappers. The way stations on the Santiam Wagon Road offered meals to weary travelers and hay for horses. By 1905, Sisters was known as a charming settlement surrounded by beautiful pine forests. Located near the foothills of the Three Sisters—three majestic snow-topped peaks—the town derived its name from this natural landmark. Sisters was formally established in 1901.

In 1870, Samuel and Jane Hindman filed the first known homestead at Camp Polk along the old military road known as the Santiam Wagon Road. The barn was on the military's former Camp Polk site. Utilizing hand-hewn logs from the abandoned military fort, he built this large barn with a way station for travelers and mail carriers to rest and care for their animals. (Courtesy of DCHS.)

In 1875, the Hindmans established the Camp Polk Post Office at their way station, where it remained until 1888, when it moved to Sisters. This post office was the only mail stop between the Willamette Valley and Prineville. Samuel operated a small store in one of the cabins left behind by the military at Camp Polk, selling supplies for travelers. Camp Polk was in the Hindman family's ownership from 1870 to 1940. (Courtesy of the Hodgers family collection.)

Martha Taylor Cobb married Charles Hindman after her husband, Alfred Cobb, died in 1898. Three generations of her Cobb family are in this buggy next to the Hindman barn. The family members are, from left to right, George Stevens; his wife, Sarah "Fannie" Cobb Stevens; their daughter, Virginia Dare "Jenny" Stevens; and Martha Taylor Cobb Hindman, the mother of Fannie and grandmother of Jenny. (Courtesy of the Hodgers family collection.)

In 1882, John B. and Elizabeth Fryrear, with their children, crossed the Cascade Mountains on the Santiam Wagon Road and applied for 160 acres on the north portion of the Camp Polk meadow along Whychus Creek to establish their homestead. The Fryrears built a house barn and dug a 20-foot well. They began irrigating 15 acres of the meadow for crops. (Courtesy of TSHS.)

In 1880, a fur trapper's cabin existed at what would become Graham Corral, southeast of Black Butte and approximately six miles northwest of Sisters. After the original cabin burned, the Stanton mill at Graham Corral provided the lumber needed to build a way station and a replacement house. Ebenezer and Ella Graham established a stopping place for travelers once they built a new home. (Courtesy DNF-SRD.)

Ebenezer Graham settled near Glaze Meadow, located at what is now the eastern portion of Black Butte Ranch, with his second wife, Ella Glines Graham, and their first child, Edwin B. Graham. Ebenezer's first wife died in California, and although Ebenezer had children from that marriage, they did not move to Oregon. Over the next eight years, the Grahams had five more children. (Courtesy of TSHS.)

12

John J. Smith filed a homestead claim in what was to become Sisters. In 1888, the post office was moved from Camp Polk to his Sisters store. He married Olive Forrest and took title to the Sisters land in 1891. In 1898, he sold it to Alex Smith, no relation. The following year, the Smiths moved to Prineville, and he was elected Crook County clerk. (Courtesy of CCHS.)

This portrait is of Robert and Eliza Smith, founders of Sisters. The town of Sisters plat map and Declaration of Dedication by Robert Smith and his brother Alex Smith were filed on July 15, 1901, and signed by John J. Smith (no relation), now the Crook County clerk. (Courtesy of DCHS.)

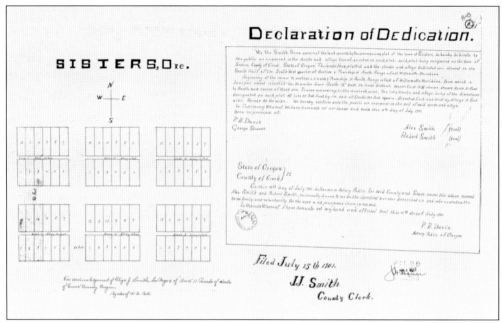

The original plat for the town of Sisters was one block north and one block south of Main Street, starting at Elm Street to the west, through Fir then Spruce to Larch Streets. Thus, the original center street through town was Main Street, although businesses built up along Cascade Street. (Courtesy of TSHS.)

In 1901, Sisters had two stores, a hotel, a blacksmith's shop, a saloon, a livery stable, and a schoolhouse. Robert Smith and Marcus J. Wilt's store carried groceries and had a small drug department. Alex Smith owned the other store in town, which became the location for the first telephone in Sisters. A hotel was constructed in 1900, initially named the Dennis Hotel, later renamed Hotel Sisters and, finally, Sisters Hotel. (Courtesy of DCHS.)

W.T.E. "Billie" Wilson, an early settler in the Sisters area, rests on a bench in front of the drugstore in 1907. This early Sisters store offered something for every shopper. Billie initially settled near Black Butte west of Sisters. He had his Wilson Steam Mill for cutting lumber on the Lazy Z Ranch a mile east of town. (Courtesy of CCHS.)

This is a view of Cascade Street in 1908 after Crook County voted itself dry. At that time, Crook County encompassed today's Crook, Deschutes, and Jefferson Counties. The "Near Beer" sign was the former Sisters Saloon, owned by George Stevens. He opened the first saloon in Sisters in the 1890s. During prohibition, he was forced to serve near beer, a fermented malt beverage containing little alcohol that was later mass-produced during nationwide Prohibition. (Courtesy of DCHS.)

Grace Cyrus Aitken was the first postmistress in Sisters, a position she held from 1912 to 1937. Grace graduated from eighth grade at Cloverdale and went to Prineville to complete her schooling at the closest high school. She started working for Robert Smith in his store in Sisters. She built herself a house and store in 1912. Later, Grace became the Sisters librarian and served for 16 years. (Courtesy of TSHS.)

Grace Cyrus and George Aitken married in 1916 and purchased the drugstore, which became known for its ice cream. They cut and stored ice in the winter to make the sought-after ice cream in the summer. George started the first newspaper in Sisters, the *Herald*. Aitken's building burned in the fire of 1923. They moved a building to the same location and were back in business the following week. (Courtesy of TSHS.)

This wagon is in front of the Sisters Post Office in the "new" one-story Aitken building following the fire of 1923. Postal service began coming through Central Oregon in 1871, and mail was delivered to Camp Polk from 1875 to 1888. When the post office moved to Sisters, the name "Three Sisters" was chosen by Jacob Quiberg, a homesteader from Sweden. The US Postal Service truncated the name to "Sisters." (Courtesy of TSHS.)

In 1909, Charles Gist remodeled this building and opened the Gist Commercial Hotel and Restaurant. Standing on Cascade Street are, from left to right, Daisy Davidson Allen, owner Hattie Gist, and an unidentified woman. The Gist Hotel burned to the ground on September 11, 1924, when a fire started in the flue, destroying buildings along both sides of Cascade Street between Fir and Spruce Streets. (Courtesy of TSHS.)

Hardy Allen was a stockman, blacksmith, and businessman born in Prineville in 1874. He homesteaded on the Metolius River, raising cattle until he moved to Sisters and started his blacksmith shop. He continued to operate the blacksmith until the 1924 fire burned his shop to the ground. Then, he built a service station at the corner of Cascade and Fir Streets in the same location as his blacksmith shop. (Courtesy of TSHS.)

Hardy Allen's Sisters Garage stood on the east end of Cascade Street and served as a blacksmith shop and community hub. The men in this photograph are, from left to right, (first row) Mose McKinney, Harvey Vincent, Warren Farthing, Charles Gist, and Peter J. Leithauser; (second row) George Wilson, Herbert McKinney, Lynn Wilson, Lester Gist, Scotty Messer, Harold Allen, Frank S. Leithauser, George Messer, Hardy Allen (leaning on the auto), and Daddy Parker. Larn Gist is in the automobile. (Courtesy of TSHS.)

Hardy Allen and Daisy Davidson married in 1900, and Hardy built this home at Main and Fir Streets. Hardy is standing at the fence, their son, Pete Allen, is sitting on it, and Daisy is standing at the gate. The Allen house was one of the finest homes of its day and is the oldest remaining original Sisters structure. The house was scheduled for demolition in the 1980s but was saved by moving it to its current location at Main and Larch Streets. (Courtesy of TSHS.)

Alfred and Martha Taylor Cobb homesteaded in 1881 and established the Cobb Roadhouse where the Lazy Z Ranch is today, 1.5 miles southeast of Sisters. The people at the Cobb barn, standing by the back fence, are, from left to right, Newt Cobb, Otis Cobb, Alfred Cobb, Martha Taylor Cobb, and John Cobb; the remaining people are unidentified. On the horse is James Taylor, Martha Taylor Cobb's father. (Courtesy of the Hodgers family collection.)

Martha Taylor Cobb Hindman was 13 when she married Alfred Cobb, and she had her first child the following year. Martha ran a way station for travelers, and Alfred was a blacksmith. Warm and generous, the Cobbs went out of their way to help others. Later, the way station building was moved to the Cyrus homestead near Cloverdale. After Alfred Cobb died in 1898, Martha married Charles Hindman. (Courtesy of the Hodgers family collection.)

George D. Taylor died on March 19, 1908, at 56 years old. He and his family arrived in Sisters in 1885 and homesteaded south of Sisters. Attending his service at Camp Polk Pioneer Cemetery are, from left to right, John B. Fryrear with his granddaughter, Martha Taylor Cobb Hindman, Sarah "Fannie" Cobb Stevens, Virginia D. Stevens, and unidentified. (Courtesy of the Hodgers family collection.)

Nettie Stuart Cobb, wife of Newt Cobb and an early settler at Black Butte, is here with her cousins. They are, from left to right, Ida Stuart, Nettie Stuart Cobb, Etta Stuart, and three cousins from the Ray Stuart family. Nettie worked in the Sisters telephone office. (Courtesy of the Kathy Kludt family collection.)

On July 3, 1880, Thomas S. Summers was the first burial in what became Camp Polk Pioneer Cemetery. He homesteaded at Sodaville, Oregon, but stayed with the Hindman family at Camp Polk, hoping his health would improve in the Central Oregon climate. He and his family had traveled over the Oregon Trail in 1845, wintering at the Whitman Mission on the Columbia Plateau, a way station on the Oregon Trail. (Courtesy of CPPCPC.)

Nellie Claypool, the second burial at Camp Polk Pioneer Cemetery, was three and a half years old when she died at the Hindmans' on November 29, 1880. Her parents, Reuben and Fannie Wilson Claypool, lived at the Fish Lake way station on the Santiam Wagon Road when Nellie became ill. They stopped at the Hindmans' when Nellie became too ill to travel farther while on their way to the closest doctor, located in Prineville, 43 miles away. (Courtesy of CPPCPC.)

This photograph was taken around 1920 from the fire lookout tree on the corner of Cascade and Larch Streets. Willis Spoo, who grew up in Sisters, identified the buildings. Some of the buildings identified by number are the Leithauser store (5), Hindman livery stable (7), John Dennis livery stable (19), Newt Cobb's barn (28), Gist Restaurant and Hotel (34), and Hardy Allen blacksmith shop (35). In the background is Black Crater Butte. (Courtesy of TSHS.)

No. 6 MAIN STREET EAST SISTERS, ORE.

Peter J. and Mary Leithauser moved to Sisters and built this two-story building, opening a barbershop with a pool table and a grocery store on the ground floor while living above on the second floor. Peter J. is standing on the sidewalk in front of his store. The Leithauser stores were a significant part of Sisters until 1977. (Courtesy of OHS.)

Frank S. Leithauser is standing on the sidewalk in front of his new store. Frank and his father, Peter J., pooled their resources and built this new store after their first store burned in the 1924 fire. Frank sold his Camp Sherman store on the Metolius River and became the proprietor of this Sisters store. This store is now the home of Sisters Bakery. (Courtesy of TSHS.)

Frank S. Leithauser stands behind the counter of his store, and Ed Greer sits on the counter. In 1941, Frank S. sold this store to his son Peter F. He moved this store a short distance east in 1950 to build the new Leithauser Supermarket on the southeast corner of Cascade and Fir Streets, which became Sisters Drug and Gift and is the current home of Habitat for Humanity. (Courtesy of TSHS.)

Lee Noonchester, a fur trapper and gold prospector who owned a ranch in Cloverdale, claimed gold was found on the McKenzie Pass at Windy Point in 1927 along with Charles Carroll of Bend. In a wild rush, 500 claims were staked in several days. Tents sprang up along the McKenzie Pass lava beds. Sisters saw a steady stream of prospectors pass through town who were lumbermen only hours before. Within a week, it was determined there was no gold, and the gold rush was over. (Courtesy of DCHS.)

Two

TRANSPORTATION OVER THE MOUNTAINS

Sisters is the gateway to two important mountain passes, the Santiam and the McKenzie. The Cascade Mountains create a natural barrier between the Willamette Valley and Central Oregon, making it challenging to reach Sisters. The building of the Santiam Wagon Road provided the first route over the mountains, leading settlers and their livestock toward the pasture lands of Central Oregon and markets in Eastern Oregon and Idaho. From 1865 to 1925, this wagon road served as the primary route across the mountains, facilitating the transportation of livestock, freight, and passengers. This played a significant role in settling Sisters by establishing a postal service and serving as a travel and commerce hub. Today, remnants of the Santiam Wagon Road are preserved in the Willamette and Deschutes National Forests, providing the longest and best-preserved stretches of any historic wagon road in western Oregon.

Reaching Central Oregon from the north was also challenging due to the Crooked River Gorge and the Deschutes River Canyon. The Columbia Southern Railroad extended south from the Columbia River to Shaniko, Oregon, in 1900, which brought the railroad closer, but it was 100 miles northeast of Sisters. In 1909, two railroad companies started building railbeds along the Deschutes River Canyon. James J. Hill's Great Northern subsidiary, the Oregon Trunk, worked on the west side of the Deschutes River, while the Des Chutes Railroad Company, owned by Edward Harriman's Union Pacific, worked on the river's east side. The competition between these two companies was fierce, including shooting at the other company's crew across the river canyon and other instances of sabotage.

Hill secured the right-of-way for a bridge across the Crooked River Gorge, built 360 feet above the river, the second-highest railroad bridge in the United States. The crossing was the only place where the cliffs on both sides were close enough to span the gorge. Famous bridge architect Ralph Modeski, the San Francisco–Oakland Bay Bridge architect, designed the bridge. On October 5, 1911, Railroad Day was celebrated in Bend, where Hill drove the golden spike. Now, Sisters had a railroad within 20 miles and a wagon road through town.

This wagon is on the Santiam Wagon Road with Mount Washington in the background. Initially, a road crew began constructing the Santiam Wagon Road with assistance from the First Oregon Volunteer infantrymen, hired to help with the final six miles to the Middle Deschutes River. At completion, travelers could go from the Willamette Valley to the Middle Deschutes Lower Bridge crossing. (Courtesy of the National Archives.)

For many years, the wagon roads were toll roads, but when toll collection stopped, the summit section through the lava beds of the McKenzie Pass Wagon Road started deteriorating. A decade later, in 1920, reconstruction of the road began, and sections were relocated and expanded. On September 21, 1925, the mountain pass section from Blue River, Oregon, on the western side of the Cascade Mountains, to Sisters was officially opened for public use, now known as Highway 242. (Courtesy of TSHS.)

John Templeton Craig was a pioneer mailman who carried mail between McKenzie Bridge on the west side of the Cascade Mountains and Camp Polk on the east side. He was caught in a sudden storm while carrying Christmas mail in 1877. He was later found by a search party frozen inside his cabin, where he died at 56 years old. (Courtesy of DCHS.)

This was the remains of the Cache Creek Toll Station on the Santiam Wagon Road in 1948. The toll station was established in 1896 fifteen miles west of Sisters with Robert Booth as the first gatekeeper. Cache Creek's locked gate blocked the way until a toll fee was paid. Gatekeepers received a monthly salary of $45, often offered lodging and meals, and operated a small supply store for travelers. (Courtesy of DCHS.)

William Fryrear was a sheep shearer and wool freighter who transported wool to The Dalles, Oregon, before the railway reached Shaniko, Oregon, in 1900. During his trips, he would drive a team of four to six horses to haul the wool and return with commercial goods. To ensure the safety of everyone on the road, horses were fitted with freight bells, prompting other wagons to make way for the freight teams as they had the right-of-way. (Courtesy of TSHS.)

Freighting outfits are at the end of the main street of Sisters in 1908. The driver of the six-horse team is riding on the left-wheel horse, and bells are on the hams of the lead teams. Sisters was a hub for replenishing supplies. Its economy flourished as stockmen and freighters passed through to mountain summer pastures to the west, winter quarters to the east, or Willamette Valley markets. (Courtesy of DCHS.)

In the early days of settling Camp Polk and the Sisters area, locals operated stagecoaches and freighting outfits. Brothers David and Joe Claypool were among the first to do so. In the 1890s, Joe ran a stagecoach and mail line on the Santiam Wagon Road from Sisters to Cascadia, Oregon, in the Willamette Valley. His goal was to deliver passengers safely and the mail on time. (Courtesy of TSHS.)

George Wilson is driving his team of horses with his hay wagon, while Peter J. Leithauser stands in the back of the wagon. Behind them is Hotel Gist, which stood at the northeast corner of Cascade and Fir Streets until 1924, when it burned. (Courtesy of TSHS.)

In 1900, Otis Cobb built a store on his ranch along Pioneer Road, which connected Sisters to Tetherow Crossing on the Deschutes River. This store was initially located on the south side of the road but was later purchased by the Cyrus family and moved to their ranch. A lean-to was added that served as the blacksmith shop while Enoch Cyrus ran the store. (Courtesy of DCHS.)

Louis W. Hill, the son of James J. Hill, the Great Northern Railroad Company president, visited Sisters in May 1910. Louis is standing on Cascade Street in front of Sisters Hotel holding a swath of red clover. When the railroad reached Bend, it served the most significant remaining portion of the United States not yet accessible by a railroad. The railroad was crucial, as it connected Central Oregon's resources with the rest of the country. (Courtesy of OHS.)

On September 17, 1911, the first train crossed the Crooked River Gorge Bridge. James J. Hill was on board to celebrate Railroad Day in Bend, Oregon. This bridge was built across a canyon 360 feet deep and 340 feet wide. It was used jointly by the Oregon Trunk Railway and Deschutes Railroad and marked the end of their race to be the first to reach Bend. The bridge was a marvel of engineering of its time. (Courtesy of TSHS.)

The Santiam Wagon Road skirted the north shore of Big Lake near Hoodoo Butte south of the summit of the Santiam Pass. A Forest Service ranger, probably Perry South, is on his horse, with a pack horse following. The lake has an elevation of 4,644 feet. It was probably named by the Andrew Wiley exploring party in 1858. (Courtesy of Steve South.)

Perit Huntington is riding his well-known donkey, Abraham. He gave many rides to children on Abraham, riding him daily to pick up the mail. Perit took a great interest in community affairs. He was artistic and entered drawings in the 1914 Sisters Fair for which he won prizes. In later years, he wrote articles about his experiences for the *Redmond Spokesman* and the *Bend Bulletin.* (Courtesy of TSHS.)

In 1914, Myrtle Gammon Dennis sits behind the steering wheel of her Dodge touring car in front of Sisters Hotel with her friend Hattie Barkman Wilt. Myrtle and her husband, John Dennis, bought Sisters Hotel in 1910. In 1912, they built the new hotel that remains in use today at the corner of Cascade and Fir Streets. The hotel had 19 rooms, heated air from the basement furnace, hot and cold water, and two bathrooms. (Courtesy of TSHS.)

On this summer day, snow lies beside the road, and the Three Sisters Mountains still have their winter coating as the stage line crosses the McKenzie Pass. Motorized stage lines replaced horse-drawn stagecoaches. Frequently, the most profitable contracts carried US mail and were competitively contested. Railroads replaced the need for individual stage companies, but stage lines over this Cascade Mountain pass remained important without an east-to-west railroad. (Courtesy of the Willitts family collection.)

The Eugene-to-Bend stage started in 1921, using the McKenzie Pass summit as one rest stop. In each direction, the remaining rest stops included Sisters, Belknap Springs, Foley Springs, and Springfield, Oregon. (Courtesy of the Willitts family collection.)

Lily Hollinshead is on a stage run on the McKenzie Pass with the Three Sisters Mountains behind her in this 1924 Studebaker Big 6. Her husband, Dean, and his two older brothers, Chet and Cecil, ran their stage lines and logging trucks from 1920 until 1942. Lily was a young schoolteacher when she came to Oregon, teaching at Redmond. After marrying Dean, she often drove for the company and was the bookkeeper. (Courtesy of DCHS.)

Four horses tow an automobile in front of Hotel Sisters on Cascade Street. Sometimes, all that a reluctant-to-start auto needed was a tow to get running again. The hotel provided shelter to numerous settlers traveling to Central Oregon on the Santiam Wagon Road. Despite the fires of 1923 and 1924, the hotel survived thanks to the citizens who hung dampened blankets out of the windows. (Courtesy of the Willitts family collection.)

Standing beside their automobile, this couple views the spectacular 9,175-foot Broken Top. Among the notable peaks in the Cascade Range, Broken Top can be seen from Sisters, particularly the Tam McArthur Rim area from South Sister to Broken Top. To the north of this rim is Three Creeks Lake, an ideal location for fishing south of Sisters. (Courtesy of DCHS.)

Mr. and Mrs. E.M. Thompson are in a Ford Model T with E.M. at the wheel and Dave Kelley in the back seat on their drive to Gist, the town closest to Sisters. Gist was founded in 1907 at the Charles Gist Ranch, which served as a post office for the area. The mail was redirected to Tumalo in 1920, and Gist became a ghost town. (Courtesy of DCHS.)

The Robert Smith General Store on Cascade Street had the first gasoline pump in town. In 1911, it started pumping gasoline using a wooden hand pump from a 50-gallon steel barrel into a gallon measuring can. At that time, the cost of gas was 50¢ per gallon, which was considered relatively high, because it had to be freighted in by horse team. (Courtesy of OHS.)

The McKenzie Pass was kept open each fall for as long as possible, as it was the only route to Eugene for many years. But the pass elevation of 5,325 feet and the narrow, twisting roadway made this problematic. In 1925, the Santiam Wagon Road route became an Oregon state highway. Then, in 1962, the McKenzie Pass route became a seasonal, scenic highway. (Courtesy of TSHS.)

Walter Hodge was a maintenance engineer for the state highway department in Redmond. His job was to keep the McKenzie Pass open for as long as possible. His family was not always happy when it snowed, which meant long hours for their father as he plowed snow from the highway that connected Central Oregon to the Willamette Valley. (Courtesy of CCHS.)

The McKenzie Pass was opened for travel each spring, usually as late as June, much as it is today. Blowing the snow and plowing the roadway from Sisters over the top of the McKenzie Pass summit could take weeks. (Courtesy of Oregon Department of Transportation.)

A new road is under construction along the Santiam River northwest of Sisters. This route was first used by explorer Finan McDonald and his party scouting for a source of beaver in 1825 for the Hudson Bay Company at Fort Vancouver. The Santiam Pass was explored for a railroad project by Col. T. Egenton Hogg, who planned to build a railroad across the Cascade Mountains. (Courtesy of Oregon Department of Transportation.)

Cars are driving west from Sisters on the new highway over the Cascade Mountains. Explorer Andrew Wiley and his party crossed the Cascade Mountains in 1859 and arrived at the area that became Sisters. From 1929 through 1931, the right-of-way for the Santiam Pass highway was logged from Sisters past Suttle Lake. (Courtesy of the Willitts family collection.)

In 1940, the Brooks-Scanlon Lumber Company started building a railroad to its holdings west of Bend. Two overpasses were built, one over the McKenzie highway about three miles west of Sisters and the other over the Santiam highway at Indian Ford. The railroad extended to Fly Creek on the western side of Big Squaw Back Ridge. The wooden trestles that crossed the highways were removed in the 1970s. (Courtesy of DCHS.)

This railroad track-laying machine is working on adding a logging spur. Four workers are in front of the boom, with others working alongside the train. The Sisters spurs ran along the eastern side of Black Butte, roughly following Green Ridge Road north from Highway 20. The western spur of the rail line cut through the area that is now Black Butte Ranch on Powerline Road. (Courtesy of DCHS.)

A Brooks-Scanlon train loaded with logging equipment crosses the McKenzie highway overpass west of Sisters hauling equipment to the logging site. After the railroad was removed, the approach embankments for the wooden railroad trestle at McKenzie Highway are still visible between the Reed Ranch and Crossroads Roads. (Courtesy of DCHS.)

Over the top of the car is the partial name "Sisters" on the rooftop of the gas station, Wakefield's Garage. This was the airmarking identifier for the Sisters Airport north of town. In the 1930s, the local airport name or identifier was added to the rooftop of a prominent nearby building. The women aviators of the Ninety-Nines Club have been airmarking since the early part of the 20th century. (Courtesy of TSHS.)

The Three Sisters mountain peaks make a breathtaking backdrop for the first runway built by Vine Stidham on the Percy Davis Ranch. In 1935, George Wakefield, who owned the Wakefield Garage in Sisters, bought the land from Vine Stidham. Wakefield built the runway with help from the Civilian Conservation Corps crew and the Forest Service. (Courtesy of TSHS.)

The view from the Sisters Airport is of the Three Sisters peaks. Maurice and Kathleen Hitchcock purchased the airstrip when they bought the Nixon farm, where they raised their family. In 1939, a flying club formed and purchased a J-3 Cub, and the first members began learning to fly. The membership included Tom Brooks, Samuel Johnson, Philip and Maurice Hitchcock, Phil Dahl, and Harold Barclay. The Hitchcocks sold the airport to Harold Barclay. (Courtesy of TSHS.)

In front of his hangar, Maurice Hitchcock is on his horse next to his Navion airplane. The runway was improved by Maurice Hitchcock when he purchased the Nixon Ranch, along with the runway, north of Sisters. (Courtesy of DCHS.)

Harold Barclay is standing next to his Cessna 120 at Sisters Airport. He was a member of the first flying club in Sisters and had purchased a Fairfield plane in partnership with George Wakefield. He built a hangar on the airport after he bought the ranch and airport from Maurice Hitchcock in 1951. Barclay supported community affairs, including clearing land for a new school and providing scholarships for high school students. (Courtesy of TSHS.)

Three

EARLY SOCIAL ACTIVITIES

Neighborly visiting among families provided most of the social life in the 1880s. As more people arrived, social life grew; picnics were held in the summer and sleigh rides and ice skating in the winter. The favorite skating place was the slough at the foot of McKinney Butte, northeast of town, where Slough Creek, later named Indian Ford Creek, overflowed. Winter sports also included skiing. The closest and earliest ski run was the Skyliners Outdoor Club at Windy Point on the McKenzie Highway, with ski jumps and a toboggan run.

At first, dances were held in homes, and later in the hall above Robert Smith's store on Cascade Street. After this hall was converted into living quarters, dances were held above Hardy Allen's blacksmith shop. Music was a vital entertainment component, with the Sisters Cornet Band and later the Sisters High School orchestra, which was established in 1936. Across from Sisters Hotel was the bandstand, with seats and a dance floor.

Rodeos were held informally and irregularly in various locations around town. The first Sisters rodeo was held in 1910 with a bucking contest at Fir and Adams Streets. In 1922, the Commercial Club sponsored the rodeo. In the 1940s, the event was relocated east of Sisters Airport. Cowboys were impressed by the high purses offered at this small rodeo, which was $500 per event, the same prize money as the big rodeos in Cheyenne, Wyoming, or Pendleton, Oregon. As a result, the rodeo was nicknamed the "Biggest Little Show in the World."

The Metolius River and Suttle Lake were popular fishing spots, as they are today. In 1923, Three Creeks Road was completed, providing access to the Three Creeks Lake south of Sisters. There were rental boats in the summer and a camping area for overnight stays.

In the 1910s, the Sisters Cornet Band gained recognition in Oregon for outstanding performances. They traveled by horseback to various Oregon locations to entertain audiences. The band had as many as 17 members, including Jesse Wilt, William A. Wilt, Jim Ship, George Wilson, Charles Gist, Clarence Wilt, Lee Zumwalt, Hardy Allen, Dick Smith, Vern Gist, Christian Sorensen, Homer Farthing, Harvey Vincent, and Roscoe Corke. (Courtesy of DNF-SRD.)

Driving the car is Fred T. Ruble, a musician and Sisters drugstore owner who sold musical instruments and was the leader of the Sisters Cornet Band. This carful of men is part of the larger band pictured at the top of the page. The bandstand was located on Cascade Street, across from Sisters Hotel. (Courtesy of TSHS.)

Clarence Wilt was an active member of the Sisters Cornet Band. He was born and raised on the family homestead in Sisters, Oregon. He was the son of John W. and Rebecca Curtis Wilt. In 1912, he and his family moved to Corvallis, Oregon, where he attended Oregon Agriculture College, now known as Oregon State University. (Courtesy of TSHS.)

Men are gathered on Cascade Street, enjoying themselves despite prohibition, with the Sisters Saloon only selling near beer, as advertised here. However, Crook County grew tired of the ban in just two years and decided to vote itself "wet" again in 1910. On the right side of the street stands Gist's Commercial Hotel, and behind the picket fence is Sisters Hotel. (Courtesy of TSHS.)

The first Sisters Fair was in October 1914. Juniper trees were cut down and placed along Cascade Street to create a festive atmosphere. The celebration lasted three days and included horse racing, agricultural exhibitions, and a baby show where a doctor from Portland examined babies. Local businesses donated prizes. The fair continued for three more years but ended due to the United States' involvement in World War I. (Courtesy of OHS.)

Frank Shaw was a Sisters Fair supporter, and the fairgrounds were located on his ranch. An old schoolhouse was moved to the ranch for exhibits. The fair lasted three days, attracting participants from across the county. The events included activities such as foot races and sheep judging, produce, and livestock entries, including the two chickens in a box on the counter with the produce entries. (Courtesy of DCHS.)

Two men stand on opposite sides of a tennis court, each holding a racket over the net. The tennis court was located east of the Belfry Church, built in 1916, which is visible in the background. The short two-plank side fences are intended to keep the ball within the court. The man standing on the right side of the court may be Pete Allen. (Courtesy of TSHS.)

A tennis player is captured in mid-air while hitting the ball. Behind the player, the tall posts with wire attached serve as a backstop for this early-day court. The backs of homes along Main Street are visible in the background. (Courtesy of TSHS.)

In 1922, Maude Cooke, a renowned adventurer and photographer from Portland, successfully summitted Middle Sister. Maude is traversing Collier Glacier, once the largest glacier in Oregon, which stretched two miles between North and Middle Sister. Today, the glacier is half its original size, measuring about one mile. Despite this, it remains a popular destination for visitors due to its gentle slope and proximity to the Pacific Crest Trail. (Courtesy of OHS.)

Hardy Allen, coach of the 1915 baseball team, is sitting on the top bleacher. The first baseball field was established in 1908 west of the Belfry Church. Baseball was popular and a big event for the entire town. The Sisters team played against Tumalo and Plainview. Elmer Ward is in the middle of the first row, with George Brewster on the far right. The top row includes Lester Gist and Edward Spoo. (Courtesy of TSHS.)

The Camp Sherman store, a tent placed over a wooden platform, was established in 1917 by Dick Fuller. In 1919, Frank S. Leithauser of Sisters bought the business, built the store, and applied to be postmaster. In 1927, the Metolius River Market Road was completed, which provided a convenient route for direct travel between Sisters and Camp Sherman. (Courtesy of DNF-SRD.)

Hanson's Resort at Camp Sherman started as a summer resort that offered tents for its overnight guests. The cabins were built in 1924, and in 1935, the resort became known as Lake Creek Lodge. The Metolius River has always been a renowned destination for fishing enthusiasts and is noted for having the nation's first and oldest "fly-fishing only" regulations. (Courtesy of TSHS.)

This 1941 rodeo parade has Carl Campbell and his young daughter Carole on their horses. Carl served as the rodeo association's president from 1947 to 1948. Carl won first place in the 1948 Quarter Horse race, and daughter Carole was named queen in 1952. In 1980, his wife, Virginia Campbell, sold the rodeo association the land that has been used as the permanent home for the rodeo ever since. (Courtesy of TSHS.)

The opening ceremonies for the 1948 rodeo featured the Cabrall family performing various horseback stunts, including this trio pyramid, with one man carrying the US flag while standing on the shoulders of the men on horseback. Louie Cabral also provided entertaining stunts, such as standing on three horses as they jumped over a gate on fire. (Courtesy of DCHS.)

Georgia Edgington Gallagher grew up on her family's ranch south of Sisters and was crowned Rodeo Queen in 1944. The rodeo queen, initially, was the young woman who could sell the most raffle tickets for a steer, but after a steer escaped one year and took two days to round up, the competition changed. The new criteria focused on horsemanship, speaking ability, and presentation skills. (Courtesy of TSHS.)

Bob Graham rode Blue Blazes, this saddle bronc, at the Sisters Rodeo in 1942. Graham was a star athlete in school, participating in basketball and track. He rode bucking horses in the early years of the rodeo; in later years, he assisted in the arena as the pickup man. In 1948, he joined the Rodeo Corporation of America. He worked for Sisters logging companies, including 18 years for Harold Barclay. (Courtesy of TSHS.)

Bob Graham on Blue Blazes.   Sisters, Ore.   June 13-14, 1942

Dot Tosta off a cow. Sisters, 1944. Photo By JeVere

In 1944, Dot Tosta, an 18-year-old cowgirl from California, was thrown off while participating in the bareback cow ride competition at the Sisters rodeo. Dot pursued her passion for being a cowgirl throughout her life. She went on to raise six children and owned a Western art gallery in Modesto, California, which she ran until the age of 89. (Courtesy of TSHS.)

Bud Travis on a Brahma Sisters 1945 Photo by DeVer

Bud Travis came from the small Central Oregon town of Terrebonne and rode this Brahma bull in the 1945 Sisters rodeo. He participated for several years and continued to be involved in the rodeo. He hand-tooled the saddle awarded to the best all-around cowboy. (Courtesy of TSHS.)

In 1948, professional rider Bob Elliott was thrown off Whizzer White at the Sisters Rodeo. Along with working horse shows, rodeo was his career. Since his home and family were in Bend, the Sisters Rodeo was a brief return home during his travels on the rodeo circuit. (Courtesy of TSHS.)

The women's Free-For-All race at the 1948 rodeo was open to all women and their mounts, requiring teamwork between the horse and rider while racing against the other participants. (Courtesy of TSHS.)

The rodeo parade, led by members of the Sisters Rodeo Association and the Ridge Riders carrying the US flag, passes by the Forest Café on Cascade Street. (Courtesy of TSHS.)

The first Skyliners lodge was established in 1928 eight miles west of Sisters on the south side of the McKenzie Highway. It had a ski run with jumps and a bobsled run that was sharp and fast. Early snow machines towed a sled with people and equipment to get to the ski area. (Courtesy of TSHS.)

In 1940, the Civilian Conservation Corps (CCC) built and completed the Santiam Ski Lodge on the Santiam Pass across the highway from Hoodoo Ski Bowl. The dormitory had enough space for 90 people to spend the night. A snowmobile operated between the lodge and Hoodoo Ski Bowl. (Courtesy of TSHS.)

The construction of Hoodoo Ski Bowl started in 1938 with assistance from the CCC. Hoodoo is situated at the peak of the Santiam Pass, west of Sisters. In 1948, a new chairlift ran from the base of Hoodoo Butte to the top elevation of 5,702 feet. This chairlift was 4,000 feet long and had an elevation gain of 1,850 feet, making it the second-largest chairlift in Oregon at the time. (Courtesy of TSHS.)

June Hauger admires the picturesque scenery from the summit of Hoodoo Butte. She was a founding member of the Oregon State Mountain Club and the giant slalom race in 1949 at Hoodoo Ski Bowl. June became an international sportswoman of exceptional skill as a world-class giant slalom racer. She competed for the Salzburg, Austria, Ski Club; won multiple International Ski Federation championships; and trained with the 1956 Austrian Women's Olympic Team while serving in the US military on European assignment. (Courtesy of OHS.)

Janice Armstrong leads her three-dog sled to the finish line at the annual sled dog races in Sisters, Oregon. The races started in 1961 and lasted through the mid-1970s, occurring in the years when there was enough snow. The races began at Hoodoo Ski Bowl and ended at the Sisters Post Office. (Courtesy of OHS.)

Four

RANCH LIFE AND WATER

The first cattle known to pass through the Sisters area was around 1862, when Felix Scott Jr. blazed a trail from the Willamette Valley over the Cascade Mountains on his way east to Idaho to supply miners. Bunch grass was abundant in Central Oregon and was welcome grazing. In 1877, John Todd had nearly 1,200 head of cattle in the area north of Camp Polk. By 1898, he had cattle ranging from Grandview to the Metolius River. By the early 1900s, cattle became an essential part of Sisters's economy, centering around the vast holdings of the Black Butte Land and Livestock Company.

The sheep industry was responsible for the growth of Sisters during the 1880s and the following decades. There were no grazing regulations in the high pastures of the Cascade Mountains; it was first-come, first-served. Since Sisters was the only settlement between the eastern sheep ranchers and the summer pastures in the mountains, it became an essential supply stop. In the summer of 1940, about 50,000 sheep pastured on the Deschutes National Forest summer range. The last sizeable sheep-raising operation in Central Oregon ended in 1969.

The Carey Desert Land Act of 1894 was the US government's support for settling the arid regions of the West. The government provided the land, up to 160 acres per homesteader, and the state would construct dams and canals to provide the water essential for prosperity. Homesteaders began arriving in Central Oregon. At the height of irrigation planning, a Suttle Lake irrigation project utilizing water in Blue and Suttle Lakes was considered. A dam 58 feet high across Lake Creek with a canal 18 miles long would bring water north of Sisters to the lower desert region near Grandview and Geneva. In 1937, the Plainview Project again proposed damming Lake Creek and building a canal. From 1912 to 1937, a total of 12 separate projects using Suttle Lake and Lake Creek water resources were considered. None of these plans materialized, leaving homesteaders without water. The lack of water caused the arid areas of Plainview, Geneva, and Grandview, among others, to be abandoned by settlers.

Black Butte, the conical peak on the western horizon, is behind the sheep in this pasture on the VU Ranch. Public land was open range for livestock grazing. This led to growing herds of cattle and flocks of sheep, which resulted in conflicts between ranchers over grazing rights. The conflicts, known as "range wars," peaked in the 1890s with vigilante attacks. In 1906, the federal government began regulating the use of public lands. (Courtesy of DCHS.)

Meredith Bailey is standing on his VU Ranch, located southwest of Sisters, around 1912. Meredith and his wife, Maida Rossiter Bailey, named their ranch for the beautiful view of the Three Sisters Mountains. The Baileys relocated from Portland to Sisters to enable Meredith to pursue his dream of running a sheep ranch. (Courtesy of DCHS.)

These photographs showcase the interior of the Meredith and Maida Rossiter Bailey ranch house on their VU Ranch. The ranch was originally homesteaded by John W. Wilt in 1892, and his brother, Marcus J. Wilt, was on the neighboring homestead. The Wilt brothers were the first to obtain water rights on Pole Creek. In 1968, Maida sold the ranch to Richard Patterson, who raised Arabian horses, llamas, and the occasional camel. Today, the ranch is known as the Pole Creek Ranch. (Both, courtesy of DCHS.)

David Clifford stands in the road amongst his flock of sheep. He emigrated from Ireland in 1920 at the age of 19 and got a job as a shepherd. He started at Silver Lake, working for Jack O'Keefe. Then he herded for Jack Shumway for 21 years on the Flume Ranch at Powell Butte. He retired when Shumway went out of the sheep business in 1972. (Courtesy of TSHS.)

Five sheepherders are inside a tent with their friend, George Stevens, on the far right, the owner of Sisters Saloon. Herding began at dawn, when the sheep started to move and graze. By mid-morning, the sheep were taken to the nearest water source. With warm afternoon temperatures, the sheep would rest and resume feeding in the late afternoon, then continue moving until dark. (Courtesy of TSHS.)

In 1905, Ellis Edgington applied for a homestead at Bull Ridge, located near Plainview southeast of Sisters. After seven years, he exchanged his Plainview homestead for a 1,200-acre ranch on Whychus Creek south of Sisters. In 1914, Ellis married Martha Crawford, a local schoolteacher, and built this log home on their ranch. (Courtesy of TSHS.)

Ellis Edgington is raking hay on his ranch. He and his wife, Martha Crawford Edgington, had four children: Jesse, Robert, Jean, and Georgia. Ellis and his friend Melvin Harrington partnered as road contractors, utilizing horse-drawn equipment to clear and level miles of roads. Later, the Edgingtons moved to a Sisters home across from the Village Green Park. (Courtesy of TSHS.)

The Sno Cap Drive-In has been serving its iconic hamburgers and milkshakes since 1954 in this very building. Its drive-up window served anyone on horseback, and in the old days, cows would pass by on their way up to the summer range. The place has remained primarily unchanged since Carl Campbell drove his cattle by on their way to greener pastures in the Cascade Mountains. (Courtesy of TSHS.)

The haying season started about the Fourth of July in the Sisters area. Central Oregon haystacks for feeding stock animals through the winter could exceed 100 tons. Each wagon was loaded by multiple men pitching hay onto the wagons while one man on the wagon spread the hay to make a well-shaped load. (Courtesy of CCHS.)

This 80-ton alfalfa haystack towers above the juniper trees on the Fred Wiese Ranch. After the last cutting, alfalfa fields became prime pasture, rented to sheep ranchers to fatten their lambs for market. In 1909, Fred married Annie Cyrus, the youngest child of Enoch and Mary Sutherlin Cyrus. (Courtesy of OHS.)

The Dennis Ranch was northeast of Sisters. John Dennis drives his harvesting team while his wife, Myrtle Gammon Dennis, and her sister, Nita Gammon Roach, stand in the field. John and Myrtle owned Sisters Hotel and erected the new building in 1912. The first building was later moved to the Dennis Ranch and became the ranch house. (Courtesy of DCHS.)

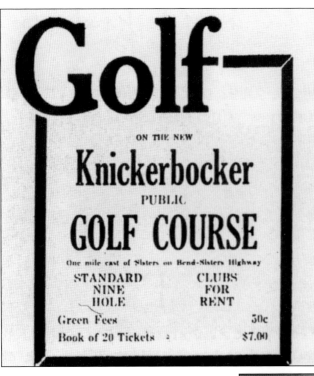

Golf—

ON THE NEW

Knickerbocker

PUBLIC

GOLF COURSE

One mile east of Sisters on Bend-Sisters Highway

STANDARD   CLUBS
NINE   FOR
HOLE   RENT

Green Fees   50c
Book of 20 Tickets $7.00

Melvin and Kitty Knickerbocker moved from their Pine Lawn Ranch to the Old Sisters Ranch in 1919. The Old Sisters Ranch was once a part of the Lazy Z Ranch south of Sisters on Highway 20. In 1931, Melvin and his brother-in-law, Hugh Amsberry, opened a nine-hole golf course on the ranch called the Knickerbocker Public Golf Course. W.G. Pringle of the Rose City Links in Portland designed the course. In 1932, an advertisement in the *Bend Bulletin* stated, "Free Turkeys, one turkey to each foursome. Details at Knickerbocker Golf Course." (Both, courtesy of DCHS.)

R. S. Everitt.   JEWELL, IA.

Kathryn Rae Knickerbocker, daughter of Melvin and Kitty Knickerbocker, is feeding the turkeys on their ranch in the winter. Other ranching families, such as the Huntingtons and Nootnagels, raised turkeys. The Huntingtons started their turkey business in 1916 and were in the industry for 34 years, while the Nootnagels raised as many as 2,000 turkeys per year in the 1920s. These ranching families raised turkeys for the Thanksgiving and Christmas markets. (Courtesy of DCHS.)

Melvin and Kitty Knickerbocker owned the Pine Lawn Ranch in Plainview around 1916. They had purchased the ranch in 1909 and sold it 10 years later. Unfortunately, the first house Melvin built on the ranch was destroyed in a fire in April 1914. However, he had a new home built by June of the same year. (Courtesy of DCHS.)

The George Cyrus family home was constructed in 1905. The Cyrus family owned a square mile of land near Cloverdale, and the Cloverdale schoolhouse was located on the northeastern corner of the section. The house was split into two sections; each piece was loaded onto a logging wagon pulled by eight horses, moved to the new site, and reassembled. Members of the Cyrus family are sitting on the front porch. (Courtesy of DCHS.)

George Cyrus was one of seven children of Enoch and Mary Sutherlin Cyrus. George is pictured here with his young family; they are, from left to right, his son George, George, LaDona, his wife Lorena Isham Cyrus, Esther sitting on her lap, and Alvin. (Courtesy of DCHS.)

The Willows Ranch was located on Indian Ford Creek north of Sisters. John Elliott rides his horse Bill while bringing in the cows. In the 1930s, the ranch had a 32-volt system with glass-covered batteries that supplied electricity for the house, milk house, and main barn. In the early years, the ranch had a lot of willows and standing water. When the swamp was drained, it became good grazing land. (Courtesy of TSHS.)

Nettie Stuart Cobb is standing with her daughter Phelma and husband, Newt Cobb, at their Cloverdale homestead in about 1910. Newt was the son of Alfred and Martha Taylor Cobb, raised on their ranch southeast of Sisters. Nettie moved to Sisters from Prineville and went to work for John J. Smith, an early Sisters homesteader and businessman. (Courtesy of the Hodgers family collection.)

Ranching on the low desert north of Sisters meant hauling domestic water long distances from Fly or Whychus Creeks. An irrigation district was bonded for $60,000 to draw water from Suttle Lake, pictured above, and Lake Creek. The Deschutes National Forest permitted the Suttle Lake Irrigation Company of Grandview to authorize dam construction. However, the state did not certify the bonds, since the project's proposed cost exceeded the assessed land value of the area. By 1916, most ranchers sold their cattle and moved out of the area. (Courtesy of CCHS.)

John B. Fryrear claimed the first water rights on Whychus Creek in 1884, building a ditch like the one in this photograph. Water rights in Oregon are governed by rules based on "first in time, first in right." According to this rule, the first irrigation districts to register their water rights can draw their maximum allotments before districts with newer rights get their water. (Courtesy of DNF-SRD.)

This cabin was at the head of the Whychus Creek canal, where water was diverted into ditches. The cabin was used by Gus Stadig when he was "riding the ditch" and was referred to as Camp Stadig. A ditch rider walked or rode horseback to inspect the creek and the ditches that took water from the stream for irrigation. (Courtesy of DCHS.)

Arnold S. Holmes worked with the Black Butte Land and Livestock Company, the largest local ranching operation, from 1900 until 1919. He traded his Black Butte company stock for the Long Hollow Ranch at Lower Bridge on the Deschutes River. The ranch had 1,500 irrigated acres and is one of the oldest ranch locations in Central Oregon. Arnold left the Black Butte company in 1918 when the Squaw Creek Irrigation District was formed. (Courtesy of Three Sisters Irrigation District.)

In 1917, the Squaw Creek Irrigation District settlers voted for $175,000 in bonds to purchase the Long Hollow Ranch from the Black Butte Land and Livestock Company, including the water rights, ditches, and diversion works. In the 1920s, the Squaw Creek Irrigation District sold bonds to raise money for capital improvements. (Courtesy of Three Sisters Irrigation District.)

Water and irrigation were the keys to successful ranching in Central Oregon. The irrigation companies were critical projects and made raising crops possible. This is the Whychus Creek Ditch Dam in 1965. (Courtesy of DNF-SRD.)

Five

LOGGING THE
PINE FORESTS

The ponderosa pine tree played a significant role in the development of Sisters and the timber industry in Central Oregon. The dense pine forests resulted in the establishment of numerous sawmills, starting in the 1880s with the small, open-air, family-run mill on a homestead. By 1930, Sisters had become a major lumber-producing town, with small sawmills powered by water or steam, many of which moved multiple times. Sisters's population grew from fewer than 200 to over 500.

The first mill on record was the Stanton mill at the old Graham Corral. Another early mill was steam-powered, built in 1890 by William Cox on the land that became the Ellis Edgington Ranch. Around 1893, this mill was bought from Cox by W.T.E. "Billie" Wilson. In 1900, Wilson purchased a steam mill and owned a waterpower mill on Pole Creek, where it became known as the Wilson Mill, powered by water from 20 acres of adjudicated water rights. The mill cut ties and timbers for the railway that was extended from Madras to Bend in 1911.

In 1906, the first mill at Plainview was established, followed by another near the Lazy Z Ranch. By 1910, Joseph Duckett and Everett Ashmore built a mill in Sisters. Several structures were built while the mill was in operation, including the new Sisters Hotel, a two-story schoolhouse, and several homes.

By 1937, six mills operated in Sisters, with a daily production of 470,000 board feet. These mills bought timber from Forest Service sales and private timber holdings. Brooks-Scanlon relocated its camp houses from Bull Springs near Tumalo in 1946. These portable camps could be moved from one site to another as the area's timber was cut. The houses were relocated west of Sisters, where Brooks Camp Road commemorates the logging camp.

The timber industry started to decline by the late 1950s, and the residents of Sisters became increasingly worried about the future of their town as mills began closing. Finally, in 1963, the last remaining mill in Sisters was closed, and it was later dismantled.

A dirt road winds through the ponderosa pine forest in the Deschutes National Forest near Sisters. Sisters is situated in a forested environment with predominantly ponderosa pines. The striking beauty of the pine forest is a classic image around Sisters. The woods were extensively cleared during the decades of logging. (Courtesy of DNF-SRD.)

The steam-powered loader on the left side of this photograph takes the logs from the "big wheel" or "high wheel" cart pulled by horses. The loader unloads and stacks the logs in piles to be transported to the mill. Big wheels were used in Central Oregon until the mid-1930s and were pulled by horses or oxen. (Courtesy of DNF-SRD.)

The slip-tongue high wheel was a logging cart with enormous wheels measuring nine to twelve feet in diameter and six inches in width. These wheels were specifically designed to efficiently transport heavy logs out of the forest. The larger diameter of the wheels ensured clearance over the logs and enabled them to roll smoothly over rough terrain. When the team descended a hill and the logs began to catch up with them, the logs were lowered to act as a brake. (Above, courtesy of DCHS; below, courtesy of DNF-SRD.)

Samuel S. Johnson, leaning against the ponderosa pine tree, graduated with a degree in forestry in 1934. He moved to Sisters, where he resided at Sisters Hotel for three years. He pursued his passion for the timber industry, managing the Johnson Company timber properties, including 40,000 acres of pine trees. Samuel owned half of Tite Knot Pine Mill with Bert Peterson and Phil Dahl, who later moved the mill to Redmond. (Courtesy of DNF-SRD.)

Hubert Van Tassel stands on a log on the millpond on his family's homestead, the Black Diamond Ranch. His job was known as a pond monkey. He is standing on a log holding a peavey, a long-handled tool used to grab the log, providing leverage to float it to a new position. Hubert's primary responsibility is to ensure the logs do not become jammed while he moves them to shore, where the logs enter the mill. (Courtesy of TSHS.)

The Dayton Mill, pictured with some of the crew, was an early Sisters open-air sawmill in which Edward Spoo was part owner. Spoo, with Joseph Duckett, started a mill in 1923, producing 25,000 board feet per shift. It included a log pond, a steam power plant, and a camp for mill workers. Spoo's wife, Hazel, cooked for the single men working at the mill. (Courtesy of DCHS.)

Edward and Hazel Templeton Spoo believed in employing their sons, Willis, Arthur, and Robert. All three sons graduated from Sisters High School and spent their summers working in the timber industry with their father. Willis continued to work for the family, and in 1938, he took over the running of the mill at Camp Polk after Joseph Duckett was bought out and the company was renamed E.H. Spoo & Sons. (Courtesy of TSHS.)

This is an open-air mill in Sisters with the workers and their families. This may be the Duckett & Ashmore Mill, located on Pine Street. In 1920, Joseph Duckett moved the mill farther north to the Steele land on Pine Street. The mill changed ownership several times, becoming the E.H.

This is the Brooks-Scanlon engine house in Sisters. In 1952, Brooks-Scanlon upgraded the railroad to Sisters. Heavier rails and treated ties were installed. On December 23, 1956, Brooks-Scanlon Inc. brought in its final load of logs by railroad on the line from Sisters. The railroad's spurs were already being pulled up when the last train of logs left Sisters Camp. (Courtesy of TSHS.)

Spoo & Sons Mill in 1932, then Hitchcock Mill in 1938. It was sold to Dant & Russell in 1951 and Leonard Lundgren in 1953. Brooks-Scanlon later purchased the mill and closed and dismantled it by 1966. (Courtesy of TSHS.)

In 1946, Brooks-Scanlon's logging camp was moved by railroad to Sisters. The camp was set up west of Sisters and named Brooks Camp. This was the last move for the Brooks-Scanlon logging camp, and it was discontinued as a company-run camp in 1956. Brooks Camp was located where The Pines community is today. (Courtesy of DCHS.)

In 1937, the work crew at the Hitchcock Mill on Sundown Ranch are, from left to right, Olie Stretzel, Dick Walters, Cecil Hitchcock, Al Helisten, Charlie Hitchcock, Francis Freeze, unidentified, Wesley Tittle, Maurice Hitchcock, Phil Hitchcock, Clifford D. Nelson, Clifford H. Nelson, Charley Bounds, Bud Winkle, Bob Culver, Orvil Hansen, unidentified, Harry

The family-owned Hitchcock Lumber Company constructed a mill in 1934 on their Sundown Ranch north of Sisters. This mill cut 50,000 feet of lumber per shift per day. The mill camp across the meadow housed the workers and their families. The timber industry benefited many people in the region who needed employment due to the dire economic conditions caused by the Depression. During that time, the Hitchcock Mill paid $4 per day. (Courtesy of TSHS.)

Woods, Samuel Bowles, Jim Bowles, Virgil Babcock, unidentified, Hal Gilbert, Jerry Winkle, and unidentified. The children in front are Richard (left) and Samuel Hitchcock (right), sons of Maurice. (Courtesy of TSHS.)

This street sign commemorates two of the numerous names in the logging history of Sisters. Both Hitchcock Lumber Company and the Leonard Lundgren Lumber Company were significant players in their years in Sisters. (Courtesy of TSHS.)

The Leonard Lundgren Lumber Company began with a portable mill in 1945 when Lundgren bought the Anthony Roach Logging Company. He moved the mill around areas of Central Oregon, including Fall River, the Fort Rock area, LaPine, the Lost Forest, Warm Springs, and a location between Indian Ford and Sisters. (Courtesy of DNF-SRD.)

In the early 1960s, when Leonard Lundgren's Sisters mill closed, Lundgren gave the library his old mill office. The closed Sisters mill stood until the 1980s. Lundgren was considered the first to mill lodgepole pine trees successfully in Central Oregon. (Courtesy of DNF-SRD.)

The camp houses are unloaded from the rail flatcars using a crane to lift them from the railroad car and place them on the ground. Two camp houses were placed together end-to-end when a larger home was necessary. Central Electric Cooperative supplied Brooks Camp with electricity, and water was run from Sisters. The children were taken to Sisters School by bus. Camp residents bought groceries in Sisters and patronized the camp's small grocery store, Scotty's Market. (Both, courtesy of DCHS.)

After the camp house is set on the ground by the crane, it is moved into place using a logging truck to maneuver the house. The area for Brooks Camp had previously been logged to make room for the 37 camp houses. (Courtesy of TSHS.)

This two-hole outhouse was moved when the Brooks-Scanlon logging camp relocated to Sisters. Several men carry the building from the railcar to set it in place. (Courtesy of DCHS.)

George and Genieve Curtis relocated to Sisters, Oregon, in 1946 when Brooks-Scanlon employed George as a truck mechanic. They stayed in Sisters for the remainder of their lives, raising their children, Harvey and Nellie. Harvey followed his father into a logging career. (Courtesy of TSHS.)

Logging railroads were constantly being moved as areas were logged off. The rails were removed from the Brooks-Scanlon railway from Bend to Sisters to Fly Creek along the Deschutes and Jefferson County line. Railroad removal started at Fly Creek on November 19, 1956, and was completed at Bend city limits on February 9, 1957. The railroads were abandoned when trucks began to haul logs. (Courtesy of DCHS.)

Barclay Logging is loading logs onto a 1942 International K-8 truck. Before the 1920s, logs were transported using wagons, but logging trucks began replacing them. The railroads were also replaced in the 1950s, and trailers were added behind the truck, allowing for a larger load of logs to be transported to the mill on each trip. (Courtesy of DCHS.)

When logging was done miles away from the mill, a vehicle, commonly known as a "crummy," was used to transport the crew from the mill to the logging site. Unfortunately, one such crummy was parked too close to the logging area, and a falling tree landed on it. The incident occurred along the old toll road west of Sisters. Luckily, no one was hurt as the bus was empty. (Courtesy of DCHS.)

Six

SCHOOLS, A LIBRARY, AND CHILDREN

Schoolhouses were community centers. Children walked or rode horseback to school, sometimes for several miles, which necessitated building schools in every community and sometimes on homesteads. The schoolhouse was used for social events such as spelling bees, church services, Sunday school, and community meetings, followed by potluck dinners and dances. The first schoolhouse near the future town of Sisters was a rural school two miles north on the Lundy Ranch, central to several early homesteads with children in the families. This rural school was established in 1883 in a hewn-log cabin.

As the town of Sisters became established, the first schoolhouse was built around 1890. As the town grew, a two-room schoolhouse was built in 1900. Then, in 1912, the increasing number of students required a new two-story, six-room schoolhouse. Initially, only two teachers were hired for the two-story schoolhouse, one for grades one through six and another for grades seven through ten. This six-room building educated the children of Sisters for 42 years. In 1923, Sisters started a four-year high school held on the second floor of the two-story schoolhouse.

The first basketball team was formed in 1923 and was ready to use the new gymnasium when it was completed in 1925. School sports were community social events, and competitors included the nearby schools of Camp Sherman, Cloverdale, Plainview, and farther away.

Other schools in the area that were also a part of the extensive Crook County school districts included Cloverdale School, built in the summer of 1900 on the George Cyrus Ranch, near that community's population center. The new Plainview School was completed in 1914 and served both the Gist and Plainview communities.

Before opening the first library in Sisters in early 1939, the Deschutes County Library left books at one of the stores in Sisters. The store proprietor was responsible for returning the books in good condition. When the Sisters branch library opened, it had room for 1,000 books on the shelves.

In 1899, seventeen students and their teacher stand before the first schoolhouse in Sisters. The school was built around 1890 and used for a decade until a two-room building, completed in 1900, replaced it. (Courtesy of DCHS.)

Another of the area's rural schools was located on William A. Wilt's homestead, about 15 miles north of Sisters near Fremont Canyon. In this class of 1914, the individuals are, from left to right, Millie Oliver, Alice Grogan, Martin Oliver, Mamie Oliver, the teacher Tillie Davidson Wilson, and Dewey Grogan. Landis Griffith is standing in the front. (Courtesy of DCHS.)

The teacher, Tillie Davidson Wilson, is in the middle of the second row in this 1911 school photograph. After Tillie married George Wilson and her twins entered school, she returned to teaching in 1923 and continued until 1961. Through her teaching, she was actively involved in the growth and development of the Sisters community. (Courtesy of TSHS.)

The two-story school building was constructed in 1912, replacing the small two-room school on the right, built in 1900. The new school had six classrooms, three on each floor. However, the second floor was not completed until 1924, when a four-year high school was added. This two-story schoolhouse served Sisters for 42 years. (Courtesy of OHS.)

In 1925, a gymnasium was added behind the two-story school, replacing the shed where students had tied their horses. The gym also served as a community center and popular venue for Sisters Rodeo dances. In the winter of 1927, the gym roof caved in from a heavy load of snow. (Courtesy of TSHS.)

The Plainview School, located six miles southeast of Sisters, was also part of the Crook County school system. Initially, there was a school at Gist, which began its operations in 1906. In 1914, a new school building was constructed at Plainview that served the communities of Gist and Plainview. (Courtesy of DCHS.)

Six children are riding Dolly, a patient and calm 30-year-old horse. The children are, from left to right, Lavelle Gray, Ladona Cyrus, Wayne Cyrus, Doris Claypool, Alvin Cyrus, and Esther Cyrus. The four Cyrus children were siblings, and Dolly likely belonged to the Cyrus family. The Cyrus and Gray families resided near Cloverdale. (Courtesy of DCHS.)

From left to right are Robert and Jesse Edgington on their horse, Dandy, and their sister, Jean Edgington, on her horse, Dolly, on their way to school. The trip to school was nearly a mile from their family's 1,200-acre Edgington Ranch southwest of Sisters on the way to Three Creeks Lake. (Courtesy of TSHS.)

Eleven-year-old Pete Allen is pictured in 1912 in this Sisters schoolroom. Pete was born in 1901 along the Metolius River at the homestead of his parents, Hardy and Daisy Davidson Allen. In 1905, Pete's parents moved to Sisters and operated Sisters Hotel and Hardy's blacksmith shop. (Courtesy of TSHS.)

Constance (left) and Kathryn Rae Knickerbocker, daughters of Melvin W. and Kitty Coine Knickerbocker, spent their early life on the family's Pine Lawn Ranch in Plainview. The sisters graduated from Bend High School and attended Oregon State College. Constance was a musician and gave piano lessons, while Rae was a teacher at the Plainview School. (Courtesy of DCHS.)

Eva and Josie Fryrear, daughters of William and Etta Fryrear, died in their youth. Eva, the eldest child, died of heart failure at 16, shortly after her marriage to George Wright. Josie, the second daughter, died at the tender age of 10. The sisters are buried at Camp Polk Pioneer Cemetery. Fryrear Butte and Fryrear Road bear their family name. (Courtesy of TSHS.)

John and Cynthia York Isham had nine children, seven of them daughters. The four Isham sisters pictured here are, from left to right, Lorena, Stella, Mary, and Viola. Lorena married George Cyrus and resided in Sisters, Black Butte, and Plainview. John Isham helped travelers pull their wagons over the McKenzie Pass, near where he homesteaded. (Courtesy of DCHS.)

In this first class of Sisters High School, the students are, from left to right, (first row) Elmer Graham and Emmett Knickerbocker; (second row) Ruby South, Aletha Hodson, unidentified, and Velma Graham; (third row) Ruby Spoo, Cecile Robbins, Ruth Spoo, Juanita Hodson, and Nellie Van Tassell; (fourth row) two unidentified, Thelma Zumwalt, Cleon Clark, and Irel Harrington. (Courtesy of DCHS.)

This 1924 Sisters High School track team was coached by the high school teacher John P. Robbins, pictured on the left. The teammates are, from left to right, unidentified, Millard Chapin, Ernie Chapin, Glen Van Tassel, and Clarence McKinney. (Courtesy of DCHS.)

In 1955, William Edwards, a Sisters teacher, instructed a group of students interested in skiing. The ski class met once a week at Hoodoo Ski Bowl. The students are gathered around the fireplace in the recreation room at the Hoodoo Lodge. The ski group named themselves "SiHyski" for Sisters High School Ski Club. Some of the students went on to serve on the Hoodoo ski patrol. (Courtesy of DNF-SRD.)

The townspeople purchased the land and built the first Sisters Library, while local sawmills donated the materials. The original building fit 1,000 books on the shelves. When it opened on January 27, 1939, the women of the Sisters Civic Club managed the library. When more space was needed, Leonard Lundgren donated an office from his sawmill in 1949. Today, this is the home of the Three Sisters Historical Society. (Courtesy of TSHS.)

The Sisters Library building was named the Maida Bailey Building for Maida Bailey, the esteemed librarian who served on the library boards in Sisters and Deschutes County; she was appointed to the Oregon State Library Board by Oregon governor Julius Meier. Maida graduated from Cornell in 1903 and worked at the Stanford library the following year. She was the founding librarian of Reed College in Portland, Oregon, in 1912 and remained there until she married Meredith Bailey in 1918. Maida is in the center, and her husband, Meredith, is on the right. (Both, courtesy of DCHS.)

The Sisters Library became a part of the Deschutes County Library on January 31, 1939, when it was officially established. The Sisters Civic Club managed the library, which received $5 per month from Deschutes County for its services. Bookmobile services were provided by the county library in Bend. (Courtesy of TSHS.)

The Cloverdale School was built in 1906 using lumber from the Dorrance Mill on Melvin Creek. In 1902, Samuel and David Dorrance started a sawmill using water from Harrison Melvin's ditch. A fatal dispute over water rights arose when Samuel blocked the ditch with sawdust. Shots were fired on December 5, 1906, resulting in the death of Samuel Dorrance. Melvin surrendered himself to the authorities the next day and was later acquitted of the charges. (Courtesy of Fáelán Lee Malay.)

High School - Grade School - Sisters Ore

In 1937, a new brick building was constructed for Sisters High School. Sisters High School was closed in 1968, and its students were bused to Redmond High School. In 1992, a new Sisters High School was constructed and opened. This brick building is now the school district administration office and was placed in the National Register of Historic Places in 2006. (Courtesy of TSHS.)

Seven

The Forest Service, the CCC, and Fire

Sisters has played a significant role in the history of Deschutes National Forest as the headquarters of the Sisters Ranger District and the short-lived Metolius Ranger District. In 1893, the Cascade Range Forest, covering 4.5 million acres, was placed under the jurisdiction of the Forest Reserves. In 1907, the name was changed to the Cascade Forest, and the Sisters district headquarters was established, located southwest of town on Trout Creek. In 1908, with the creation of the Deschutes National Forest, Sisters remained the headquarters of the Sisters Ranger District.

Camp Sisters, a Civilian Conservation Corps (CCC) Camp, was established in 1933, during the Great Depression. It was a temporary summer camp until the permanent base was built in 1934. By 1940, Oregon had 61 CCC camps and several thousand young men working in the forests. The CCC provided employment and training to young men aged between 17 and 23. Their work included building forest roads, reducing fire hazards, fighting fires, and constructing fire lookouts, trails, and campgrounds.

Sisters suffered several devastating fires. On May 11, 1923, a fire started in an unoccupied garage on Cascade Street. The fire destroyed buildings on the south side of the street, including 10 businesses and residences, one of which was the Aitken's Drug Store and post office. The records burned with the offices housed in the Aitken building, including Squaw Creek Irrigation District and the US Forest Service. Sisters Hotel came dangerously close to destruction. Few people were in town during the fire, since many residents were attending a track meet in Redmond. Then, 16 months later, on September 11, 1924, a fire started in a defective flue in the Gist Hotel on the north side of Cascade Street, burning buildings on both sides of the street. Sisters Hotel was saved by townspeople who soaked blankets and sheets with water and draped them over the exterior of the building. Firefighters from Bend, Redmond, and the Forest Service responded, with ranger Perry South directing the firefighting efforts.

A 110-foot-tall ponderosa pine tree located at the intersection of Cascade and Larch Streets became one of the earliest fire lookouts in the Sisters Ranger District in 1915. Harvey Vincent, a Forest Service employee, and E.H. Howell, deputy state fire warden, built an 80-foot-tall lookout from the tree. (Courtesy of DNF-SRD.)

Iron rungs, made by Hardy Allen's blacksmith shop, were installed to create the ladder. A platform with three enclosed sides was constructed at the top of the tree. The lookout tree was cut down in 1926 after it died and began to rot, which made it unsafe. (Courtesy of DNF-SRD.)

This photograph was taken from the fire lookout tree following the September 11, 1924, fire in downtown Sisters; the white building on the right is Sisters Hotel. Across from the hotel is the new Wakefield Garage. South, across Cascade Street, is a new gas station, but the Leithauser Grocery and Parker & Company stores are gone, having burned in the fire. (Courtesy of TSHS.)

Perry South is with his wife, Leda Graham South, with Carl on her lap in the backseat of their automobile. In the front are Ruby and Marion, who is "driving" the car. Leda was the daughter of Ebenezer and Ella Graham, born and raised at Graham Corral. The Perry South Campground on the Metolius arm of Lake Billy Chinook is named for him. (Courtesy of Steve South.)

Perry was appointed a forest guard in 1906 and became an assistant ranger on the Cascade North National Forest in 1907. Soon after, he was the first ranger in the Metolius District. In addition to his ranger duties, he also served as the director of Sisters School. After retiring, he operated a stock ranch in Grandview. (Courtesy of Steve South.)

These Forest Service employees from the Sisters District include, second from left in the front row, ranger Perry South. The others are unidentified. Perry was the first ranger in charge of the Metolius District and served as a US Forest Service ranger for over 30 years. (Courtesy of Steve South.)

Allingham ranger station   4/6/16

The first building constructed on the Deschutes National Forest was the Allingham Guard Station on the Metolius River. Bob Pyett built a small cabin and occupied the site in 1880. In 1888, he traded the property to David W. Allingham. He built the house in 1890, selling it in 1900 to Mr. Alley, who later reconveyed the title to the government. Ranger Perry South lived at the ranger station starting around 1906. (Courtesy of Steve South.)

The Dee Wright Observatory was built of native lava to provide shelter for the many travelers who stop to visit and view the major mountain summits visible from this location. The circular tower allows the mountain summits to be observed through wall openings. The structure honors Dee Wright, a longtime guide, trail builder, CCC foreman, and horse packer for the US Forest Service. (Courtesy of DCHS.)

Two of the Three Sisters Mountain peaks are viewed from this opening in the Dee Wright Observatory on the McKenzie Pass. The CCC at Camp Sisters constructed the Dee Wright Observatory in 1935 amid 65 square miles of lava fields. (Courtesy of DCHS.)

This Forest Service gathering includes the following employees and family members: in the first row, second from the left is Leo Henries, third is Carl South, sixth is Marion South, eighth is Archie Brown, and ninth is Perry South. Standing in the second row, eighth from left, is Leda Graham South. (Courtesy of Steve South.)

Camp Sisters, the CCC camp, was established in 1933 upstream from Camp Sherman on the east bank of the Metolius River. Camp Sisters was one among several camps established in the central Cascade Mountains during the Depression years, including Seven Mile Hill, Camp Crane Prairie, and Camp Belknap. (Courtesy of OHS.)

This is the album cover of the scrapbook compiled as a record of the CCC camps within the Eugene District. The scrapbook contains photographs, maps, and data for each camp within the district. (Courtesy of OHS.)

Camp Sisters's management is, from left to right, camp superintendent Gordon Marsh, chief officer Lieutenant Parks, camp surgeon Lieutenant Vermillion, and foreman Cleon Clark. Cleon was from the Sisters Ranger District Office and had been in the first graduating class of Sisters High School in 1924. He became the assistant superintendent and later the superintendent of Camp Sisters. (Courtesy of OHS.)

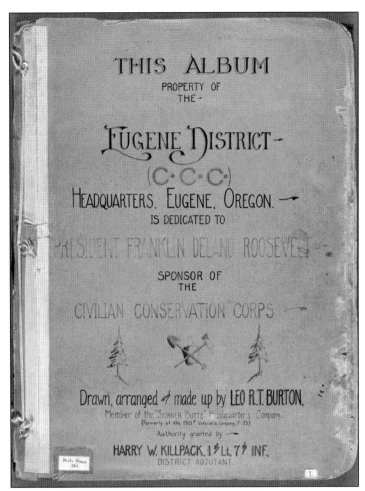

Camp Sisters began as a temporary camp with only tents as shelters. The camp was closed in the fall of 1933 and reopened in the spring of 1934, becoming a permanent camp and replacing the tents with bunkhouses. Camp surgeon Lieutenant Vermillion's youngest sons, Joe (left) and Dick (right), visited Camp Sisters in 1933. (Both, courtesy of OHS.)

The construction of the Trout Creek Butte fire lookout tower west of Sisters was begun in 1933 by the CCC at Camp Sisters. It was an 86-foot steel tower with a 7-by-7-foot cab as the lookout at the top. More than 500 cubic yards of concrete were used to build the abutments for the tower. The tower was constructed for a total expense of $1,654. A nine-mile-long telephone line was strung from the Forest Service headquarters in Sisters to the Trout Creek Butte lookout. Fires were discovered earlier with more lookout towers in service and improved communication methods. (Both, courtesy of OHS.)

The Trout Creek Butte lookout dwelling was constructed near the tower's base in 1934. A 14-by-16-foot living quarters cabin and a 16-by-18-foot garage were built. The Forest Service often hired women as fire lookouts who occupied the towers throughout the summers. (Courtesy of OHS.)

A CCC employee builds a fire line around the Moore Creek Fire in the Deschutes National Forest in July 1933. The CCC men were essential firefighters throughout that summer. The summer was hot and dry, and no significant rain fell for several months. Oregon set forest fire records that remained in place for over 80 years. (Courtesy of OHS.)

This barren section of the Santiam Wagon Road was the location of a lightning-caused fire fought by the Camp Sisters CCC men in 1936. This section is along Seven Mile Hill. (Courtesy of DNF-SRD.)

The first building erected by the US Forest Service for the Sisters Ranger District was located at the corner of Elm and Washington Streets. It served as an office, weather station, and where fire information was telephoned from the lookout towers. (Courtesy of TSHS.)

This 1957 photograph of US Forest Service employees was taken in front of the Sisters Ranger District Office of the Deschutes National Forest with the fleet vehicles behind them. Among the men are Skip Ashman, Gordon George, Rolly Ludwig, Joe Clyde, Bob Wright, Fred C. Hoin, Mike Nesbitt, Randall McCully, and Phillip McCully. (Courtesy of DNF-SRD.)

George Wakefield owned and operated the Wakefield Garage in Sisters and worked with the Forest Service and the CCC. He kept his automobile collection in the carriage house behind his home. He started the Sisters Airport in 1936 with the help of the Forest Service and the CCC men at Camp Sisters. (Courtesy of TSHS.)

In June 1960, a fire broke out in George Wakefield's garage and Chevron gas station on Cascade and Fir Streets. Embers spread across the street to the Leithauser Supermarket and Variety Store. The Wakefield Garage was a complete loss. (Both, courtesy of DCHS.)

In 1950, the Leithauser family built this modern supermarket at the southeast corner of Cascade and Fir Streets. The first Leithauser store, built in 1911, burned down in the fire of 1924. Their second store is visible at the far left of this photograph, and today, it is Sisters Bakery. Their third store, Leithauser's Supermarket, was damaged in June 1960 by the fire that broke out across the street at the Wakefield Garage. (Courtesy of TSHS.)

NASA officials searched for a suitable location for a training ground for Apollo astronauts, selecting the lava beds west of Sisters in the Deschutes National Forest. On the right is Deschutes National Forest supervisor Ashley A. Poust discussing the training area with NASA. The other men are, from left to right, John Slight, space engineer; Dr. William Feddersen, crew performance, Space Medicine Branch; and Earl LaFevers, test director. (Courtesy of the National Archives.)

In this August 1964 photograph, astronaut Walter Cunningham sits on a pickup tailgate on the McKenzie Pass in a pressurized space suit while technicians prepare for maneuverability tests. Cunningham went on to pilot the lunar module on Apollo 7 in 1968. (Courtesy of the National Archives.)

Using a stabilizing lunar walker and wearing a pressurized suit, Randolph H. Hester walks down a slope of lava rock on the McKenzie Pass Lunar Surface Training Site while crew members follow wearing coveralls. The other men are, from left to right, E.V. LaFevers, crew systems space medicine; Curtis Mason, advanced spacecraft technology geologist; and R.D. Wiladson, crew systems, Apollo Support Division. (Courtesy of DCHS.)

Eight

BUILDING A FUTURE

By the 1950s, Sisters residents became concerned about the town's future as mills closed or moved out of the area. The last sawmill closed in 1963, and Sisters High School closed in 1968, with the students bussing to Redmond. The first overnight automobile court, Sorensen's, was built on the corner of Fir and Cascade Streets in 1924. In later years, the Sisters Motor Lodge was built, and by 1960, eight gas stations were servicing the tourists that passed through town.

Capital from the lumber industry began to fuel the development of destination resorts. During the 1960s, Brooks-Scanlon formed Brooks Resources, a land development subsidiary of the lumber company that developed several recreational properties, including Black Butte Ranch.

Sisters was a mixture of architectural styles resulting from the rebuilding after the back-to-back fires of 1923 and 1924, which included the 1950s taverns, the cottage style of Days Café, and the remains of a few false fronts from the town's beginnings. Discussions began about enacting an ordinance requiring a uniform facade for commercial buildings. This was encouraged by Brooks Resources, who wanted an appealing town for their new residents and tourists at Black Butte Ranch. In 1978, an ordinance was passed, and buildings along Cascade Street created the storefront look that existed during the settling of Sisters.

Only two lights were left on at night in town in the early years. One was at Farleigh's Service Station and the other at Jesse Wilt's Sisters Hotel. Both businesses operated power plants to keep the lights on. As tourism developed, during the summers and hunting seasons, some bars and cafés would take turns staying open all night to ensure no one was ever stranded. Sisters became that small-town welcoming community that worked to maintain friendly charm while the cultural vitality was enhanced through events that enriched the lives of all who visited.

The Public Works Administration replaced the wooden sidewalks on Cascade Street in 1937. Then, in June 1951, streetlights were installed, and the following week, the street was paved from sidewalk to sidewalk by a state highway crew. In the 1960s, the side streets were paved. (Courtesy of TSHS.)

The Gammon sisters pose in front of the Knickerbocker-Eyerly house in Sisters. Throughout their lives, they played important roles in the Sisters community, owning businesses, supporting the schools, operating sawmills, and offering employment. They are, from left to right, Nettie Gammon Tewalt Templeton, Myrtle Gammon Dennis, Ethel Gammon Hitchcock, Vivian Gammon Russell, Nita Gammon Roach, and Lois Gammon Bush. (Courtesy of TSHS.)

Five men are socializing in the afternoon sun in downtown Sisters. They are, from left to right, Mose McKinney, Peter J. Leithauser, W.T.E. "Billie" Wilson, and two unidentified men. These men were early settlers of Sisters, with McKinney building the first fire lookout on Black Butte, Leithauser building and operating his family-owned grocery stores in Sisters for 70 years, and Wilson starting one of the first sawmills in the area. (Courtesy of TSHS.)

Walking in the snow on Cascade Street, the Forest Café is on the left, and the Sisters Cascade Theatre is on the right. The Forest Café sported unique architecture with its rounded, all-glass front and an impressive neon sign with a red arrow. It was built in 1924 by Roy M. Rickert of the Rickert Mill, located on the Redmond Highway. (Courtesy of the Willitts family collection.)

Sorensen's Auto Camp was established in Sisters to accommodate the increasing number of travelers. It was added behind the first-ever service station in town, built in 1924 on the south side of Cascade Street between Fir and Elm Streets. The camp was comprised of 15 modern cabins with carports attached to each, forming a courtyard or U-shape around the Shell station. Chris Sorensen worked on improving and expanding cabins until he passed in 1940. His wife, Mary Ridenhour Sorensen, managed the business until 1966. The auto camp boasted oil-heated "modern" cabins. The phone number to reach them was 971. (Both, courtesy of the Willitts family collection.)

The Sisters Motor Lodge was built in 1948 and featured a garage next to each room for traveling motorists. The original owner, Ruth Chapin, developed the motor lodge but sold it after only three years. A brilliant neon sign was added in the 1950s to beckon the increasing number of tourists passing by on the McKenzie Highway. (Courtesy of TSHS.)

On September 28, 1954, this photograph was taken from the Chevron station looking west on Cascade Street, showing the Santiam Service Station, Sno Cap Drive In, and electric poles with streetlights. Across the street is Johnson's Sporting Goods, the Hancock service station, and Sisters Motor Court. (Courtesy of Central Electric Cooperative Inc.)

In 1949, in the early days of the Central Electric Cooperative (CEC), line crews string power lines in Sisters. Before CEC, Langman Electric Company generated electricity one mile north of Sisters. However, in 1941, CEC replaced the private plant by running an electrical transmission line from nearby Redmond. Central Electric Cooperative line crews work on a streetlight in front of Sisters Hotel in 1949. (Both, courtesy of Central Electric Cooperative Inc.)

Looking west along Cascade Street, Sisters Hotel is on the right with the Cascade Café, its food-to-go, and Budge & Irene's Tavern. Next is the empty lot with a for sale sign where the Owl Tavern previously stood; last is Bush's Market, owned by Clyde and Lois Gammon Bush. Clyde served as the mayor of Sisters for several years. (Courtesy of TSHS.)

This little café started as the Pondosa Café in 1934. It became Ladd's Café around 1945, owned by Arthur and Ethel Cain Ladd. The next owner, Neil Winkle, moved the building a short distance to the west, enlarged it, named it Ruth's Café, and added the Wink Room bar. In the 1970s, it became the Gallery Restaurant, where local artist Ray Eyerly held court daily on his bar stool and where his paintings in the Western tradition adorned the walls. (Both, courtesy of TSHS.)

Ray Eyerly is pictured beside one of his paintings featuring the Three Sisters in the Gallery Restaurant, where his artwork has been displayed since 1963. He worked as a wheat farmer, sheepherder, ranch hand, and cowboy. Sisters was his chosen hometown, and Ray became an internationally recognized American West artist. He was the first artist to be honored by the Oregon State Legislature. (Courtesy of DCHS.)

Sisters Rodeo Association attracts nearly 30,000 people to Sisters for the five-day rodeo each June. It offers quality rodeo stock and high purses, guaranteeing the best in the sport. In 1988, the Sisters Rodeo Association was accepted as a member of the Professional Rodeo Cowboys Association, the "Big Daddy" of professional rodeo, indicating the fine reputation Sisters built over 80 years of quality rodeo. (Courtesy of TSHS.)

On a summer Saturday in 1975, Jean Wells Keenan proudly displays a collection of 12 quilts she and her grandmother had handmade. This exhibition has since become an annual tradition in Sisters, showcasing the town's unique blend of art, nature, and inspiration. The Sisters Outdoor Quilt Show displays over 1,200 quilts and attracts more than 10,000 visitors. (Both, courtesy of TSHS.)

In the early 1890s, the Black Butte Land and Livestock Company was established. It operated five ranches, including Swamp Ranch, now known as Black Butte Ranch. This area was renowned for its excellent grazing. However, the company dissolved in 1918. In 1969, Brooks Resources began developing Black Butte Ranch. Destination resorts like Black Butte Ranch fall within CEC's service territory. (Courtesy of Central Electric Cooperative Inc.)

The Sisters Folk Festival is the annual three-day music festival "where all the town's a stage," presenting a broad spectrum of Americana and roots music, including folk, bluegrass, gospel, old-time, and rhythm and blues. Established in 1995 by Jim Cornelius and Dick Sandvik, the festival is produced at a multitude of venues throughout the city. (Courtesy of TSHS.)

BIBLIOGRAPHY

Brogan, Phil F. *East of the Cascades.* Portland, OR: Binfords & Mort, Publishers, 1964.

Deschutes County Historical Society. *History of the Deschutes Country in Oregon.* Bend, OR: 1985.

Felt, Margaret Elley. *Maurice G. Hitchcock: The Flying LumberJack.* Bend, OR: Maverick Publications, 1985.

Hatton, Raymond R. *Oregon's Sisters Country: A Portrait of Its Lands, Waters and People.* Bend, OR: Geographical Books, 1996.

An Illustrated History of Central Oregon; Embracing, Wasco, Sherman, Gilliam, Wheeler, Crook, Lake and Klamath Counties, State of Oregon. Spokane, WA: Western Historical Publishing Company Publishers, 1905.

Lent, Steve. *Central Oregon Place Names: Volume II, Jefferson County.* Prineville, OR: Crook County Historical Society, 2008.

———. *Central Oregon Place Names: Volume III, Deschutes County.* Prineville, OR: Crook County Historical Society, 2015.

McArthur, Lewis A. *Oregon Geographic Names.* Portland, OR: Oregon Historical Society Press, 1992.

Morisette, Martin Gabrio. *Green Gold: The Incomplete, and Probably Inaccurate, History of the Timber Industry in Parts of Central and Eastern Oregon from 1867 to Near the Present.* Post, OR: 2005.

Nielsen, Lawrence E., Doug Newman, and George McCart. *Pioneer Roads in Central Oregon.* Bend, OR: Maverick Publications, 1985.

Vaughan, Thomas, ed. *High & Mighty: Select Sketches about the Deschutes Country.* Portland, OR: Oregon Historical Society, 1981.

Williams, Elsie Horn, for Bend Chamber of Commerce. *A Pictorial History of the Bend Country.* Norfolk, VA: The Donning Company Publishers, 1983.

Wilson, Tillie, and Alice Scott. *That Was Yesterday.* Redmond, OR: Midstate Publishing, 1976.

Winch, Martin. *Biography of a Place: Passages through a Central Oregon Meadow.* Bend, OR: Deschutes County Historical Society, 2006.

INDEX

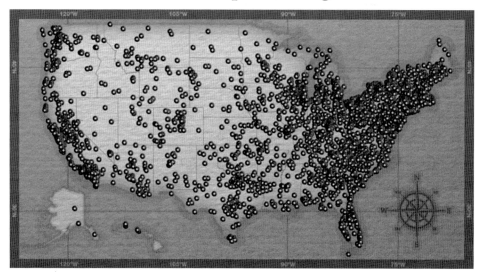